CHARTER AND BY-LAWS,

OF THE

NEW YORK HISTORICAL SOCIETY.

C. Shields, Printer.

THE

CHARTER AND BY-LAWS

OF THE

NEW YORK HISTORICAL SOCIETY.

REVISED MARCH, 1846.

[SECOND EDITION, WITH AMENDMENTS TO JANUARY 1853.]

NEW YORK:
PRINTED FOR THE HISTORICAL SOCIETY.

M DCCC LIII.

NEW YORK:
PRINTED BY CHARLES SHIELDS.
23 PLATT STREET.

Officers of the Society, 1853.

PRESIDENT,

LUTHER BRADISH.

FIRST VICE PRESIDENT,

THOMAS DE WITT, D. D.

SECOND VICE PRESIDENT,

FREDERIC DE PEYSTER.

FOREIGN CORRESPONDING SECRETARY,

EDWARD ROBINSON, D. D.

DOMESTIC CORRESPONDING SECRETARY,

JAMES W. BEEKMAN.

RECORDING SECRETARY,

MAUNSELL B. FIELD.

TREASURER,

WILLIAM CHAUNCEY.

LIBRARIAN,

GEORGE HENRY MOORE.

EXECUTIVE COMMITTEE.

AUGUSTUS SCHELL, Chairman.
MARSHALL S. BIDWELL,
BENJAMIN H. FIELD,
FRANCIS L. HAWKS, D. D.,
JOHN ROMEYN BRODHEAD,
ERASTUS C. BENEDICT,
ANDREW WARNER.

GEORGE H. MOORE, Secretary.

[The officers of the Society are members, *ex officio*, of the Executive Committee. The Society's Rooms are in the University Building, and are daily open to the members. Stated meetings of the Society on the first Tuesday of the month.]

At a meeting of the New York Historical Society, held at their Rooms on Tuesday Evening, the 17th March, 1846, Mr. Bradish offered the following resolution, submitted by the Executive Committee, which was adopted:

Resolved, That the By-Laws adopted by the Society, be referred to the Executive Committee, with instructions to have prepared and printed, in pamphlet form, the original Act of Incorporation of the Society, the Act of 1826 reviving that Act, the Act of 1846, reviving and amending the original Act of Incorporation, the existing Act of Incorporation as revived and amended, the By-Laws, and a list of officers and members of the Society.

Extract from the Minutes.

ANDREW WARNER,
Recording Secretary.

At a meeting of the Executive Committee of the New York Historical Society, held at the Library, on Tuesday Evening, April 20th, 1852,

On motion of Col. Warner, it was resolved that the subject of a new edition of the Charter and By-Laws of the Society and the Register of Members, be referred to the President and Librarian, with power.

Extract from the Minutes.

GEORGE H. MOORE.
Secretary.

ORIGINAL ACT OF INCORPORATION.

AN ACT

To incorporate the New York Historical Society: Passed February 10th, 1809.

WHEREAS, the persons hereinafter named, and others, have formed themselves into an association under the name of "The New York Historical Society," for the purpose of discovering, procuring, and preserving whatever may relate to the natural, civil, literary, and ecclesiastical history of the United States in general, and of this State in particular, and have presented a petition to the Legislature to be incorporated, that thereby such, the purpose and design of the said Society, may be the more effectually subserved and promoted. Therefore,

1. BE IT ENACTED BY THE PEOPLE OF THE STATE OF NEW YORK, REPRESENTED IN THE SENATE AND ASSEMBLY, That Egbert Benson, Brockholst Livingston, Benjamin Moore, Samuel Miller, William Johnson, Samuel L. Mitchell, David Hosack, John M. Mason, DeWitt Clinton, John McKesson, Anthony Bleecker, Charles Wilkes, John Pintard and John Forbes, and their associates, who now are, and such other persons as shall hereafter become members of the said Society, shall be, and are hereby ordained, constituted and declared a body corporate and politic, in fact and name, by the name of "The New York Historical Society," and that by such name they and their successors forever hereafter shall and may have succession, and by the same name be capable in law to sue and be sued, plead and be impleaded, answer and be

answered unto, defend and be defended, in all courts of law and equity, in all manner of actions, suits, complaints, and matters whatsoever; and that they and their successors may have a common seal, and the same break, alter, change, and renew at their pleasure, and by the same shall be forever hereafter capable in the law to purchase, take, hold, receive, and enjoy, to them and their successors, any lands, tenements, hereditaments, goods, chattels or estate, real or personal, of whatever nature or quality in fee simple, for life or lives, or for years, or in any other manner whatsoever: provided always, that the yearly income or value of the said real or personal estate do not at any time exceed the sum of fifteen hundred dollars, current money of the State of New York.

2. AND IT IS HEREBY FURTHER ENACTED, That they and their successors by the same name, shall have power and authority to give, grant, bargain, sell, demise, release, and convey to others the whole or any part of such real or personal estate on such terms, and in such manner and form as the said Society may deem eligible to subserve and promote such, the purpose and design of the said Society, and that they and their successors shall have power from time to time, to abolish any of the offices or appointments hereinafter mentioned, and create others in their room, with such powers and duties as they may think fit to confer and prescribe, and shall have power from time to time to make, constitute, ordain, and establish such constitutions, by-laws, ordinances and regulations as they shall judge proper for the election of officers, the election and admission of new members for the government and regulation of the officers and members, for fixing the times and places of the meetings of the said corporation, and for conducting, regulating, and managing all the affairs and business of the said corporation, and the same from time to time to alter, change, repeal, revoke, and annul at their pleasure; and that the constitution and by-laws, rules and regulations of the said Society heretofore made and adopted, and now existing, shall and may remain in force until altered or repealed by the said corporation: provided, that such by-laws, constitutions and regulations made or to

be made by the said corporation shall not be repugnant to the constitution and laws of the United States or of this State.

3. AND BE IT FURTHER ENACTED, That the officers of the said Society, until otherwise ordained by the said corporation, shall consist of one President, two Vice Presidents, a Correspondent Secretary, a Recording Secretary, a Treasurer, a Librarian, and standing Committee of seven members, and that until the next annual meeting of the said Society, and until others shall be chosen in their places, the present officers and committees last appointed by the said Society, shall be and continue respectively the officers of the said corporation.

4. AND BE IT FURTHER ENACTED, That this act shall be, and is hereby declared to be, a public act, and shall be construed most favorably to subserve and promote such, the purpose and design of the said Society, and that no misnomer of the said corporation, in any deed, will, testament, gift, grant, demise, or other instrument of contract or conveyance, shall vitiate or defeat the same, provided the said corporation shall be sufficiently described to show the intention of the parties.

5. AND BE IT FURTHER ENACTED, That this act shall be and remain in full force for the term of fifteen years: provided, nevertheless, that in case the aforesaid Society shall at any time appropriate their, or any part of their funds to any purpose or purposes other than those contemplated by this act, and shall be thereof convicted by due course of law, that thenceforth the said corporation shall cease and determine, and the estate, real and personal, whereof it may be seized and possessed, shall vest in the people of this State.

REVIVAL OF THE ACT OF INCORPORATION.

AN ACT

For renewing and continuing in force an Act entitled, "*an Act to incorporate the New York Historical Society.*" *Passed February* 10, 1809. *Passed February* 10, 1826.

1. BE IT ENACTED BY THE PEOPLE OF THE STATE OF NEW YORK, REPRESENTED IN THE SENATE AND ASSEMBLY, That the act entitled, "an act to incorporate the New York Historical Society," passed February 10, 1809, shall be, and the same is hereby revived and extended and continued in force until the tenth day of February, which will be in the year of our Lord one thousand eight hundred and thirty-nine: And the said act shall be taken and considered to have been in full force and effect, since the time of the passing thereof, in the same manner as if the same had not expired by its own limitation.

2. AND BE IT FURTHER ENACTED, That the officers last appointed by the said Society or Corporation, pursuant to the provisions of the said act shall be, and continue to be officers of the said Corporation, till others shall be duly chosen in their respective places: And the estate and property which the said Society or Corporation may have legally acquired, or which they may legally hold, pursuant to the said act, they may continue to hold, and may convey and dispose of the same, in the same manner as if the said act had always continued in full force and effect.

REVIVAL AND AMENDMENT

OF THE

ACT OF INCORPORATION.

AN ACT

To revive and continue in force an Act entitled, "an Act to incorporate the New York Historical Society," Passed February 10, 1809, *and to amend the same. Passed February* 2, 1846. *By a two-third vote.*

THE People of the State of New York, represented in Senate and Assembly, do enact as follows:

1. The Act entitled "an Act to incorporate the New York Historical Society," Passed February 10th, 1809, is hereby revived and continued in force.

2. The said act so revived and continued in force, is hereby amended by striking out at the end of the first Section thereof the words, "Provided always that the yearly income, or value of the said real or personal estate, do not at any time exceed the sum of fifteen hundred dollars, current money of the State of New York;" And inserting in the place thereof the words: "but the clear yearly income of the said real and personal estate, over and above the Library and collections of the said Society, shall not at any time exceed the sum of ten thousand dollars."

3. The said revived act is hereby further amended, by striking out in the fifth line of the third Section thereof the words, "A correspondent Secretary," and inserting in the

place thereof the words, "A foreign corresponding Secretary, and domestic corresponding Secretary."

4. The said revived act is hereby further amended, by striking out in the first part of the fifth Section thereof the words, "That this act shall be and remain in full force for the term of fifteen years: Provided nevertheless."

5. The Legislature may at any time alter or repeal this act.

6. This act shall take effect immediately.

THE CHARTER.

The Charter of the New York Historical Society, as revived, continued in force and amended, February 2d, 1846.

WHEREAS, the persons hereinafter named, and others, have formed themselves into an Association, under the name of "The New York Historical Society," for the purpose of discovering, procuring, and preserving whatever may relate to the natural, civil, literary, and ecclesiastical history of the United States in general, and of this State in particular, and have presented a petition to the Legislature to be incorporated, that thereby such, the purpose and design of the said Society, may be the more effectually subserved and promoted:

Therefore,

§ I. BE IT ENACTED BY THE PEOPLE OF THE STATE OF NEW YORK, REPRESENTED IN THE SENATE AND ASSEMBLY, That Egbert Benson, Brockholst Livingston, Benjamin Moore, Samuel Miller, William Johnson, Samuel L. Mitchell, David Hosack, John M. Mason, DeWitt Clinton, John McKesson, Anthony Bleecker, Charles Wilkes, John Pintard and John Forbes and their associates who now are, and such other persons as shall hereafter become members of the said Society, shall be, and are hereby ordained, constituted, and declared a body corporate and politic, in fact and name, by the name of "The New York Historical Society," and that by such name they and their successors, forever hereafter shall and may have succession, and by the same name be capable in law to sue and be sued, plead and be impleaded, answer and be answered unto, defend and be defended, in all courts of law and equity, in all manner of actions, suits, complaints, and matters whatsoever; and that they and their successors may have a common seal, and the same break, alter, change, and renew at their pleasure, and by the same be forever hereafter capable in the law to purchase, take, hold, receive, and enjoy, to them and their successors, any lands, tenements, hereditaments, goods, chattels or estate, real or personal, of whatever nature or quality, in fee simple, for life or lives, or for years, or in any other manner whatsoever; but the clear yearly income of the said real and personal estate, over and above the Library and collections of the said Society, shall not at any time exceed the sum of ten thousand dollars.

§ II. And it is hereby further enacted, That they and their successors, by the same name, shall have power and authority to give, grant, bargain, sell, demise, release, and convey to others, the whole or any part of such real or personal estate, on such terms, and in such manner and form as the said Society may deem eligible to subserve and promote such, the purpose and design of the said Society; and that they and their successors shall have power from time to time to abolish any of the offices or appointments hereinafter mentioned, and create others in their room, with such powers and duties as they may think fit to confer and prescribe, and shall have power from time to time to make, constitute, ordain, and establish such constitutions, by-laws, ordinances, and regulations as they shall judge proper for the election of officers, the election and admission of new members, for the government and regulation of the officers and members, for fixing the times and places of the meetings of the said corporation, and for conducting, regulating, and managing all the affairs and business of the said corporation; and the same from time to time to alter, change, repeal, revoke, and annul at their pleasure; and that the constitution and by-laws, rules and regulations of the said Society heretofore made and adopted, and now existing, shall and may remain in force until altered or repealed by the said corporation: provided that such by-laws, constitutions and regulations, made or to be made by the said corporation shall not be repugnant to the constitution and laws of the United States, or of this State.

§ III. And be it further enacted, that the officers of the said Society, until otherwise ordained by the said corporation, shall consist of one President, two Vice Presidents, a Foreign Corresponding Secretary, a Domestic Corresponding Secretary, a Recording Secretary, a Treasurer, a Librarian, and standing Committee of seven members; and that until the next annual meeting of the said Society, and until others shall be chosen in their places, the present officers and committees last appointed by the said Society shall be and continue respectively the officers of the said Corporation.

§ IV. And be it further enacted, that this act shall be and is hereby declared to be a public act, and shall be construed most favorably to subserve and promote such, the purpose and design of the said Society, and that no misnomer of the said Corporation, in any deed, will, testament, gift, grant, demise, or other instrument of contract or conveyance shall vitiate or defeat the same: provided the said corporation shall be sufficiently described to show the intention of the parties.

§ V. And be it further enacted, that in case the aforesaid Society shall at any time appropriate their, or any part of their funds to any purpose or purposes, other than those contemplated by this act, and shall be thereof convicted by due course of law, that thenceforth the said Corporation shall cease and determine, and the estate real and personal, whereof it may be seized and possessed, shall vest in the people of this State.

§ VI. The Legislature may at any time alter or repeal this act.

§ VII. This act shall take effect immediately.

BY-LAWS.

NAME.

I. THE name of this Society is, "The New York Historical Society."

OBJECT.

II. The object of the Society is to discover, procure, and preserve whatever may relate to the natural, civil, literary, and ecclesiastical history of the United States in general, and of the State of New York in particular.

MEMBERS.

III. The Society shall consist of Resident, Corresponding, and Honorary Members. Resident Members shall be persons residing in the City of New York, or its immediate vicinity within this State. Corresponding and Honorary Members shall be persons residing elsewhere; and not more than twelve Honorary Members shall be elected in any one year. Resident Members upon removing from this City or its immediate vicinity, and on giving notice thereof to the Recording Secretary, shall thereafter be Corresponding Members; and, in like manner, Corresponding Members upon coming to reside in this City, or its immediate vicinity, shall cease to be Corresponding Members; and, upon giving the like notice, shall thereafter be Resident Members.

IV. Members shall be elected as follows: The candidates shall be proposed publicly at a meeting of the Society by a member thereof; and the nominations, together with the name of the member making them, shall be entered on the minutes, and be referred to the Executive Committee. The Reports of that Committee recommending candidates for election, shall be openly read to the Society, at a meeting subsequent to that at which the nominations were made; and if any member demand a ballot, the election shall be by ballot, and three black balls shall exclude. If no ballot be demanded, the candidates so recommended, shall be declared duly elected members of the Society.

ANNUAL FEES AND DUES.

V. Each resident member shall pay, on admission, an initiation fee of FIVE DOLLARS, and FIVE DOLLARS annually, as dues; or, in lieu thereof, a life membership fee of FIFTY DOLLARS, as a commutation for all the regular dues and fees: provided, that in all cases of election after the summer recess, the dues to be charged to members so elected, for the remainder of the year, shall be for six months only, or TWO DOLLARS and FIFTY CENTS. Should any resident member, other than a life-member, fail to pay the said annual fees and dues for two years successively, or at any time refuse to pay the same, the Executive Committee shall have power to erase his name from the list of members, and he shall no longer be a member of the Society.*

OFFICERS.

VI. The Officers of the Society are—

A PRESIDENT,
A FIRST VICE PRESIDENT,
A SECOND VICE PRESIDENT,
A FOREIGN CORRESPONDING SECRETARY,
A DOMESTIC CORRESPONDING SECRETARY,
A RECORDING SECRETARY,
A TREASURER, and
A LIBRARIAN.

* As amended, May 2, 1848.

They shall be elected annually by ballot, and shall hold their offices respectively for one year, and until others shall be chosen in their places.

These officers, together with seven other members, to be appointed annually by the President, shall constitute a standing Committee, to be called "The Executive Committee."

ANNUAL MEETING.

VII. The Society shall hold an annual meeting on the first Tuesday of January in each and every year hereafter, at which a general election of officers by ballot shall take place. In such election, a majority of the ballots given for any officer shall constitute a choice: but if, on the first ballot, no person shall receive such majority, then a further balloting shall take place, in which a plurality of votes given for any officer shall determine the choice.

Whenever the first Tuesday of January shall be the first day of January, the annual meeting above provided for shall be held on the Wednesday following.

VACANCY.

VIII. If a vacancy shall happen in any of the offices of the Society, it may be filled by special election, at a regular meeting of the Society; and the person so elected to fill a vacancy, shall hold his office for the unexpired term of his immediate predecessor in office, and until another shall be elected in his place.

MONTHLY AND SPECIAL MEETINGS.

IX. The Society shall meet regularly for the transaction of business, at its rooms, on the first Tuesday in every month, unless otherwise specially ordered. But the President, or, in his absence, either of the Vice Presidents, may, and upon the written request of any five members, shall call a special meeting, giving three days notice thereof, to be published in at least two public newspapers, printed in the City of New York.

ORDER OF BUSINESS.

X. At the regular meetings of the Society, the following shall be the order of business:

1. The reading of the minutes of the last meeting.
2. Reports and communications from officers of the Society.
3. Reports of the Executive and other Committees.
4. Election of members previously proposed.
5. Nomination of new members.
6. Miscellaneous business.
7. Papers read, and Addresses delivered, before the Society.

ANNIVERSARY.

XI. On the third Tuesday of November in each year, being the anniversary of the founding of the Society, there shall be an address delivered before the Society by the President, or some other person to be appointed for that purpose by the Executive Committee.

QUORUM.

XII. At all meetings of the Society, twenty-one members shall constitute a quorum for the transaction of business.

PRESIDING OFFICER.

XIII. The President, or, in his absence, one of the Vice Presidents, or, in their absence, a Chairman pro tempore, shall preside at all meetings of the Society, and shall have a casting vote. He shall preserve order, and shall decide all questions of order, subject to an appeal to the Society. He shall also appoint all Committees authorized by the Society, unless otherwise specially ordered.

CORRESPONDING SECRETARIES.

XIV. The Corresponding Secretaries shall conduct the general correspondence of the Society. They shall have the custody of all letters and communications to the Society, excepting papers read, and addresses delivered before the same, which shall be deposited in the Library. They shall, at every meeting of the Society, read such letters and communications as they may have received; they shall prepare all letters to be written in connection with the business or objects of the Society, and transmit the same; but the Society may appoint a Committee to prepare a letter or letters, on any special occasion. They shall notify all members of their election, and of such other matters as they may see fit, or shall be directed by the Society; and shall transmit to them their proper diplomas, or certificates of membership. They shall keep, in suitable books to be provided for that purpose, true copies of all letters written on behalf of the Society; and shall carefully preserve the originals of all letters and communications received.

The duties of the Foreign Corresponding Secretary shall be limited to the correspondence with individuals or associate bodies in foreign countries; and those of the Domestic Corresponding Secretary shall, in like manner, be confined to the United States, except that, in the absence of either of these officers, or during a vacancy in either office, its duties shall be performed by the remaining incumbent, until such absence shall terminate, or the vacancy be supplied.

RECORDING SECRETARY.

XV. The Recording Secretary shall have the custody of the Seal, Charter, By-Laws, and Records of the Society. He shall, under the direction of the President, or either of the Vice Presidents, give due notice of the time and place of all meetings of the Society, and attend the same. He shall keep fair and accurate records of all the proceedings and orders of the Society; and shall give notice to the several officers, and to the Executive and other Committees, of all votes, orders, resolves, and proceedings of the Society, affecting them, or appertaining to their respective duties.

TREASURER.

XVI. The Treasurer shall collect and keep the funds and securities of the Society. Out of these funds, he shall pay such sums as may be ordered by the Society, or by the Executive Committee. He shall keep a true account of his receipts and payments; and, at each annual meeting, render the same to the Society, when a Committee shall be appointed to audit his accounts.*

XVII. If from the annual Report of the Treasurer there shall appear to be a balance against the Treasury, no appropriation of money shall be made for any object but the necessary current expenses of the Society, until such balance shall be paid.

LIBRARIAN.

XVIII. The Librarian, in connection with the Executive Committee, shall have the charge and superintendence of the rooms, and the custody and arrangement of the books, manuscripts, and other articles belonging to the Library and collections of the Society. He shall cause to be prepared and kept, a proper catalogue and list of the same. He shall acknowledge the receipt of donations to the Society in his department. He shall expend in the purchase of books and other articles, and for their safe keeping and preservation, with the approbation of the said committee, such sums of money as shall from time to time be appropriated for that purpose, and report thereon to the Society. He shall, at least once in each year, render his accounts for such purchases and expenditures, to the Treasurer for settlement, and shall further make to the Society, at each annual meeting, a full report on the condition and progress of the

* As amended March 5, 1850.

Library and collections. He shall have power to employ, at a salary to be fixed by the Executive Committee, an Assistant Librarian, who shall be under his direction, and perform such duties as he may assign; and who, during the hours at which the Library is open, shall be always present.

LIBRARY REGULATIONS.

XIX. The following shall be the regulations for the use of the Library:

1. No book or manuscript shall at any time be lent to any person to be removed from the Society's Rooms.
2. No Manuscript in the Library, nor any paper read before the Society and deposited in its archives, shall be published, except by the direction of the Society, or with the consent of the Executive Committee.
3. The hours during which the Library shall be open, shall be determined from time to time, by the Executive Committee.
4. During such hours, any members of the Society may have free access to consult any book or manuscript, except such as may be designated by the Executive Committee, and to make extracts from the same under the authority of the Librarian. Any person not a member, may obtain the like privilege of consultation from the President or Librarian, if known to them, or upon the recommendation of some other member, to whom the applicant is known. But no person not a member, shall be permitted to take extracts from the manuscripts of the Society, excepting the donors or depositors of the same, without special authority from the Executive Committee.
5. It shall be the duty of the Librarian, or his Assistant, to report to the Executive Committee any injury done to any book or manuscript by any person consulting the same; and the said Committee may, at their discretion, lay such Reports before the Society. For any

such injury, the person doing it shall make such pecuniary compensation as the said Committee shall judge proper; and if he be not a member, the Committee shall have power, if they think fit, to prohibit him from further access to the Society's Rooms.

EXECUTIVE COMMITTEE.

XX. It shall be the duty of the Executive Committee to solicit and receive donations for the Society; to recommend plans for promoting its objects; to digest and prepare business; to authorize the disbursement and expenditure of unappropriated monies in the hands of the Treasurer, for the payment of salaries, current expenses, fitting up the Library, the ordinary purchase of books, binding, printing, and other necessary outlays.

They shall, in connection with the Librarian, have charge of the arrangement and regulation of the Library and collections; and shall have authority at any time to examine into the condition of the same, and into the state of the finances; as also generally to superintend the interests of the Society, and execute all such duties as may from time to time be committed to them by the Society. At each annual meeting of the Society, they shall make a general report. Except during the summer vacation of the Society, they shall meet regularly for the transaction of business, once at least, in every month; and if any member of the Committee, not an officer of the Society, shall be absent from its meetings for three successive months, without reasons therefor satisfactory to the Committee, his place on the Committee shall be vacated, which fact shall be reported by the Committee to the Society, and the President shall proceed immediately to fill the same by a new appointment.

At all meetings of the Executive Committe, five members shall constitute a quorum for the transaction of business.

XXI. The Executive Committee shall provide a suitable case or cases, to be placed in the rooms of the Society, for the deposit and safe-keeping of all papers and other things belonging to the department of the Foreign Corresponding Secretary, the Domestic Corresponding Secretary, the Recording Secretary, the Treasurer, the Librarian, and the Executive Committee. And all papers and other things belonging to each of these several departments respectively, shall be deposited and constantly kept, by its proper officer, in the case or cases appropriated for its use, under his special care and upon his official responsibility.

NUMBER OF MEMBERS ON COMMITTEES.

XXII. All Committees of the Society, other than the Executive Committe, shall be composed of three members, unless otherwise specially ordered.

ALTERATION OF BY-LAWS.

XXIII. No alteration in the By-Laws of the Society shall be made, unless such alteration shall have been openly proposed at a previous meeting, and entered on the minutes, with the name of the member proposing the same; and shall be adopted by a majority of the members present at a regular meeting of the Society.

www.ingramcontent.com/pod-product-compliance
Lightning Source LLC
LaVergne TN
LVHW011143110826
845150LV00008B/2489

* 9 7 8 1 4 1 8 1 9 2 7 5 4 *